P9-EDS-636

Fire in the Night

The Life and Legacy of

Fr. Paul

of Graymoor

✛

3-19-14

Seed of Fire in my heart burn strong & true.

Fr Jx

Joseph Scerbo, S.A., Ph.D.

✛✛✛✛✛

The life and legacy of Father Paul of Graymoor,
pioneer for Christian unity and reconciliation,
apostle of charity, international leader,
champion of the Church, ardent Franciscan, torch-bearer

Table of Contents

Dedication

Everything we own, we owe, said a wise man. There are two individuals in my life to whom I owe much. The first is Franciscan Sister of the Atonement Alexis Joseph Zeitz, S.A. I first met her when I was seven years old. She prepared me for First Holy Communion, enrolled me as a "knight of the altar," and taught me to serve Mass with reverence and wonder. Her love for the Society of the Atonement affected me deeply. She was prayerful, insightful, and full of fun, and she saw in me someone "special." She fed me constantly with books about the lives of the saints, giving me many role models of holy and courageous people.

The crypt chapel in St. Anthony's Shrine at Graymoor
(pictured c. 1950s), where Fr. Paul was laid to rest

Sr. Alexis Joseph and the other Sisters of the Atonement were loved by the people of my home town, Mechanicville, New York. I and many others are deeply grateful for the formative influence these sisters had upon our lives and purpose.

It was Sr. Alexis Joseph who introduced me to my first Atonement friar, Fr. Adrian Ramanauskas, S.A., who would later be one of my professors at St. Pius X Seminary, Graymoor (1961-65). This very educated and eloquent friar guided me during my years of college and philosophy studies.

The second person to whom I am particularly grateful is Fr. David Gannon, S.A., who introduced me to writings on the mystical life. My first exposure to St. John of the Cross, St. Teresa of Avila, and other contemplative giants came from Fr. Gannon's guidance. I owe him much.

Perhaps I owe him even more gratitude because he accepted the assignment made by Fr. Angelus Delahunt, S.A., to write the first biography of Fr. Paul James Francis Wattson. Each day as he passed Fr. Paul's tomb, in St. Anthony's Shrine, or on his way to offer the Holy Sacrifice of the Mass, Fr. Gannon pleaded for Fr. Paul's prayers before the throne of Infinite Wisdom. He sought to present the founder of Graymoor to the world in a fitting and realistic way. Fr. Gannon completed his task with the first biography eleven years after the death of Fr. Paul. In writing *Fire in the Night*, I have drawn substantially upon Fr. David's informative and insightful work. Therefore, I dedicate my efforts herein to Fr. David Gannon, S.A.

I would also like to acknowledge the excellent works of Fr. Fred Alvarez, S.A., on the life of Fr. Paul, preserved in the Graymoor Archives. In *Prophet of Reunion: The Life of Paul of Graymoor*, Charles Angell, S.A., and Charles LaFontaine, S.A., provide a perceptive portrait of the founder and trace the Society up to 1975. Likewise, this book benefits from the biography of Mother Lurana White by Sister Mary Celine Fleming, S.A., *A Woman of Unity.*

I could not have completed this work without the generous assistance of Graymoor archivist Barbara Martire, who is distinguished by her deep knowledge of the Society and by her love for the founders. I must also express gratitude to Mary-Cabrini Durkin, my indefatigable editor, for her support and guidance.

Minister General Fr. James Puglisi, S.A., asked me to pull together—in a much shorter form—some key moments in the life and legacy of Fr. Paul. This pioneer for Christian unity had a broad vision and a long reach. This apostle of charity, ardent Franciscan, champion of the Church, reconciler, international leader, and missionary's heart touched the world in a Christ-like way.

I pray that my readers may be inspired by the life-call of Fr. Paul and respond to the grace of God as he did. May they follow *their* unique call in the crises of *their* lives to improve the world around them in the spirit of the Gospel.

The entire purpose of Fr. Paul's life was to work and pray for the realization of Christ's prayer at the Last Supper: "That they all may be one; as thou, Father, art in me, and I in thee, that they also may be one in us…" (John 17:21). This unity surely would fulfill the prayer which Jesus recommended to his disciples, "Thy kingdom come, thy will be done, on earth as it is in heaven."

On a pilgrimage to the ecumenical French monastery in Taizé, I was blessed by the grace of a conversation with its founder, Brother Roger, whom Pope Benedict described as a "tireless witness to the Gospel of Peace and ecumenical reconciliation, a pioneer in the difficult paths towards unity among the disciples of Christ." It was Taizé that inspired Pope John Paul II to initiate World Youth Day. Brother Roger's eyes shone with piercing intensity as he spoke to me a heartfelt message, simple and profound: "Work for Christian unity with everything you have, with your whole self!" I find no better call for my own life. May Christians in dialogue deepen the communion that already binds them! One day, may full visible unity in sacramental life, witness, and the apostolic faith be shared in the Holy Spirit's Pentecostal power!

I pray that this modest introduction to Fr. Paul Wattson and Mother Lurana White may be used by God to draw others into the ranks of bridge-builders, peace-makers, and reconcilers.

Friar Joe Scerbo, S.A., Ph. D.

Foreword

It is with great pride and joy that I present this popular work on Paul Wattson, SA, Founder of the Franciscan Friars of the Atonement, who together with Lurana White, SA, co-founded the Society of the Atonement.

Perhaps he is best known by the mark he left on the religious history of the 20th century as being the initiator of what is now known as the Week of Prayer for Christian Unity. He was likewise one of the key figures in the founding of the Catholic Near East Welfare Association, which aids Christians of the Oriental Churches. In addition, his prophetic vision that created the Union-that-nothing-be-lost (UNBL) continues to aid the poor, missionaries, and laborers for Christian unity well beyond its foundations in the beginning of the last century. The countless homeless men who pass though the doors of St. Christopher's Inn can attest to the charitable heart burning in this humble man. They find refuge and solace in the home of the Friars. Many of those coming there today suffer from addictions of various kinds.

In *Fire in the Night*, it is my hope that women and men will discover the person of Paul Wattson, his outstanding Christian virtues and heroic efforts to overcome the alienation of sin that has divided Christians for centuries. He is, as Fr. Scerbo describes him, a builder of bridges, an ambassador of reconciliation, a true Franciscan. His love of the poor, of God's good creation but, most of all, of the supreme self-gift of God's only Son in the atonement on the cross animated Paul Wattson's entire life. In this Fr. Paul of Graymoor is an authentic witness of God's continuing concern that all of creation find its true purpose for which it was made, to find *shalom*, that abiding peace where Creator and creature are at one in the heart of God.

May these pages inspire you to be engaged in the search to fulfill Christ's prayer for the unity of his followers as witnesses to the unity of the Triune God and the truth of the Gospel. Each in his or her own way can be an ambassador of reconciliation, as was Fr. Paul, by seeking to live the spirit of the Beatitudes, by doing justice, loving kindness and walking humbly with God (Micah 6:8).

V. Rev. James F. Puglisi, SA
Minister General
Feast of St. Anthony of Padua

Preface

Light a candle in a dark room and watch as the light instantly overcomes the darkness. Observe the power and grace of that single solitary flame dancing with life!

Now light another candle and feel the hope it brings.

Now light several candles from the first two and experience the added warmth, illumination, and comfort they give. The Easter Vigil begins in darkness with this sign: the light of Christ passed from the Paschal candle, from one person to another through the congregation. Both Fr. Paul and Mother Lurana of Graymoor were living flames of God's desire for unity in Christ's Body, the Church. In the words of Pope Benedict XVI, "Restless in the dark, we grow together in the Light."

Fr. Paul knew well the darkness that hangs over many a prophetic soul. Self-doubt and spiritual anguish plagued him, and not only in the early years of his vocation. Even as God confirmed his path, he suffered blows such as alienation from friends and colleagues and charges of disloyalty and mental imbalance. Assaults from all sides included downright lies and came even from a few within the Society of the Atonement.

Sometimes our fire is extinguished. Spirit-knit friends re-kindle that flame, as Francis and Clare and Fr. Paul and Mother Lurana did for each other.

Torch-bearers come in all forms. There is the Statue of Liberty in the New York Harbor which welcomed my immigrant Italian father when he was eleven years old. There is the Olympic torch that is carried every four years when the world comes together for athletic games.

Then there are living lights and leaders of movements. There is the torch which lit the Peace Corp volunteers as President John F. Kennedy received the baton which had been passed to the next generation. Pope John XXIII called the Second Vatican Council, and the Holy Spirit's Pentecostal flame reignited the Church. Fr. Paul lifted the torch for the unity of Christians, and the healing of divisions that had rent the garment of Christ.

In the United States of America, God raised up two souls with a passion for Church unity in the spirit of St. Francis of Assisi. The lives of Fr. Paul Wattson and Mother Lurana White and the birth of the Society of the Atonement are testaments to an undying passion. This passion stems from the heartbeat of Jesus himself, and his prayer at his Last Supper, "That they all may be one; as thou, Father, art in me, and I in thee, that they also may be one in us..." (John 17:21).

Mother Lurana White

The passion of Christ for unity is a heart-felt energy that flows through us, not from us. It is the energy that carries us on our life's journey. From Love we come—to Love we go!

Miracles happen when we allow the passion of Christ for unity to flow through us.

Fr. Paul Wattson

May the life of Fr. Paul spark your imagination to develop new symbols of ecumenism! May your own life story become a bridge for restoring broken trust and renewing Church unity!

When you feel passionate and inspired about something or someone, what is your frame of mind? What are you willing to do? What kind of effort are you willing to put forth? What are you willing to do to turn your vision into reality? How do you lean forward and bring your passion, skill and intensity to the canvas of life? What is the role of holy silence in allowing you to listen for your responsibility for this world that we all share?

Journey

O God, thou hast taught me from my youth...

Psalm 71:17

We all journey. The road from birth to final breath is mapped within a perfect plan known only to God. Some reach promise. Others fall along the way. The truly fortunate discover two special gifts.

First, they come to a true understanding of themselves in humility and truth—as they are before their Creator. This understanding counts no position or property.

Second, they discover their Creator as their very life, breath, and being. They come to know themselves in him, their mission as a part of His greater mission, and their identity as members of the family of God.

The pattern of journey frames the life and legacy of Fr. Paul James Francis of the Atonement. He took the path marked out by God and discovered the truth of himself and of his relationship with God. The Society of the Atonement, its works, and myriad personal transformations stand in testimony to the authenticity of his journey.

The following chapters will explore the most important themes and developments along Fr. Paul's and Mother Lurana's journeys.

Fr. Paul's journey was fueled by Jesus' passion for Unity "that they all may be one." His journey invites us to ask, "How do I find God's path for me? What is God's plan for my life?"

Like Fr. Paul, like Francis of Assisi, like all the saints, we too discover God's call through each situation in life. The Holy Spirit offers unexpected new life even when everything seems to be bleak. **Conversion involves allowing the events of your life to change your perspective.** Fr. Paul understood his need for an on-going change of heart and for an on-going change of perspective **that allowed him to see from God's point of view.** Let us use our imaginations to perceive what the eyes cannot yet see.

The painter Paul Gauguin claimed he shut his eyes in order to see; perhaps he was saying that the heart sees what the eyes cannot.

Close your eyes and see!

1

Chapter One

The Journey Begins

> *It is you who light my lamp;*
> *the LORD, my God, lights up my darkness.*
>
> *Psalm 18:28*

Is there a time in human history without darkness, strife, division, or trouble? No, not since the Fall.

Envy, sin, and self-will divided the first two brothers. The result was murder, exile, and suffering for all concerned.

Into such a world was our founder born.

Fr. Paul of Graymoor was born Lewis Thomas Wattson to Reverend Joseph Wattson and Mary Electa Wattson. On January 16, 1863, Lewis saw the light of day and felt the warmth of love. But on that day, and many more to come, his country suffered strife, division, death, darkness, and war. It was the time of America's Civil War, with its horrible slaughter and wholesale destruction.

As Reverend Joseph Wattson and his wife knew well, this Civil War brought a special torment. Though Lewis was born in Millington, Maryland, in the Union, the family had recently moved there from the Confederate state of Mississippi.

A pastoral call to Maryland was welcomed by this Episcopal priest and his wife. It was a call away from pain, poverty, prejudice, and the punishment of war. Amid sorrow and want, the family joined other refuges trekking through the mud and across the Yazoo River. They were among the few to have an ox cart. Lewis's mother would never let him forget their story and struggle. She encouraged in him a thankful heart for the life he would come to know in Maryland.

Some accept conflict and suffering with hopeless resignation: "Why try?" But Fr. Paul would face darkness and divisions with hope, believing in One who said, "You are the light of the world."

Rev. Joseph Wattson, 1887, father of Lewis

Mary Electa (née Gregory) Wattson, mother of Lewis

A Preaching Vocation

Lewis Wattson's keen sense of humor and independent mind were a chip off the old block! His father had once been accused of being a "Jesuit in disguise" because of a joking remark to a seminary classmate. Following in Rev. Joseph Wattson's footsteps, the son entered The General Theological [Episcopal] Seminary in New York.

Lewis Wattson aged 21

Lewis's first intimation of a preaching vocation had been sparked by his father's remark that the Episcopal Church needed a preaching order like the Paulists. His father was an effective preacher, and here too Lewis took after him. This gift became apparent when the young man was ordained an Anglican deacon in 1885, and one year later a priest. Scripture and the Church Fathers fired his sermons. He preached the power of the Holy Spirit and the redemptive love of Jesus, the Crucified and Risen One. His passion about Jesus Christ's desire for unity made him an animated and notable public speaker. As he grasped a cross which hung from his neck, his resonant words flowed from his own heart and touched many other hearts. The promise of Jesus was realized, that "If you believe in me, from your heart shall flow a stream of living water."

Trusting the Holy Spirit to inspire him, Lewis began to write in 1894 in his parish publication, *The Pulpit of the Cross*. Self-described by its author as "aggressive rather than defensive," *The Pulpit of the Cross* treated topics such as the Divine Presence, unconditional

*Lewis T. Wattson
in 1882,
when he graduated from
St. Stephens College,
presently Bard College*

*Holy Innocent Episcopal Chapel of St. Stephen College,
Annandale-on-Hudson, New York*

love, and the forgiveness of sins. From the viewpoint of Scripture and history, Lewis saw the Pope, the Bishop of Rome, as the Vicar of Christ on earth. His thinking was undergoing a radical change from his firm belief in Anglo Catholicism. Where would his sincere and honest searching lead him?

As the rector of St. John's Episcopal Church in Kingston, New York, Lewis grew in his desire to found a "preaching order" like the Paulist priests. The Spirit continued to goad him. Should he retire to a monastery…? Restless was his heart until he found his place in God's larger plan. The Gospel-based life of St. Francis of Assisi touched him deeply.

A preaching order associated with the passion and death of the divine Redeemer—God would bring this dream to life through Lewis. Imitating the method of St. Francis in seeking divine guidance, he opened the Scripture three times in honor of the Blessed Trinity.

St. John's Episcopal Church, Kingston

First Atonement Text – Holy Spirit

The day was July 9, 1893. After a morning communion service which he celebrated with intense fervor, Lewis took down from the pulpit the King James Version of the Bible. Holding the inspired word in his hands, he knelt. With fervent expectancy, he invoked the Holy Spirit and opened the Scriptures three times.

The first passage he opened to, John 7:37-39, would ever remind him of the graces of the Holy Spirit, which would pour forth as living water and satisfy his spiritual thirst.

> In the last day, that great day of the feast, Jesus stood and cried, saying, If any man thirst, let him come unto me, and drink. He that believeth on me, as the scripture hath said, out of his belly shall flow rivers of living water. Now he said this about the Spirit...

The transformation of every new generation of friars would flow from this grace. Indeed, thirst and holy desire mark the beginning of all spiritual life.

Later Lewis would find that Lurana White shared this thirst, expressed in one of her favorite scriptures: *"As a deer longs for flowing streams, so my soul longs for you, O God"* (Ps 42:1). Lewis would find in Sr. Lurana a kindred spirit. But where would this desire for God lead them? St. Francis' primary exhortation to his followers guided both of them: *"Follow the Holy Spirit and His Holy Manner of working!"*

Romans Chapter 5
"...we joy in God through our Lord Jesus Christ, by whom we have now received the Atonement."

Fr. Paul's notations of the three scripture passages he received on July 9, 1893

✝

Society of the Atonement.

Jesus promises the Holy Ghost
S⁺ John VII, 37, 38. 39

The Mystery of the Atonement.
Romans V. . 8, 9, 10, 11, ✝ 19, 20. 21.

The Atoning Sacrifice
1 Cor. . XI. 23, 24, 25. 26, 27, 28, 29.

In Nomine Patris, et Filii, et Spiritus
Sancti. Amen —

Given from Heaven 6ᵗ Sunday after Trinity
July 9ᵗ 1893.

Second Atonement Text – At-one-ment

As Lewis opened the Bible for a second time, St. Paul's words in the Letter to the Romans were a lightning bolt that electrified his long yearning to found a preaching order like the Paulists:

We joy in God through Our Lord Jesus Christ, by whom we have now received the Atonement (Rom 5:11).

The Atonement! (The word can be found only in the King James Version. In other translations the word *reconciliation* appears.) The theological concept of atonement refers to the birth, life, passion, death and resurrection of Jesus. It describes how humanity can be reconciled. Christ succeeds in **undoing** the wrong (sin) that Adam committed. United with humanity, Christ leads his brothers and sisters into eternal life.

Sin is forgiven; humanity is delivered from slavery to Satan; the heart is set on the right track to moral change. The mystery of the Atonement means that we have been initiated into a great liberation. In a far distant future, Fr. Paul would remind his spiritual sons and daughters that "JOY is the keynote" of their vocation, the joy that comes from being at-one with God and others through the reconciling love of Jesus Christ.

"Atonement" expresses both the spiritual gift and the mission of the Society, which he later explained as follows:

> The Latin "adunatio" etymologically is exactly the same as the English "atonement," the root words being ad and unus, in English at-one… It was by our Lord's sacrifice on the cross that an at-*one*-ment, or reconciliation, was made between God and man,

and the union of God and man in the person of our Lord Jesus Christ at His Incarnation made possible for the elect by His sacrifice on Calvary. The central text of our Institute, which contains the word 'atonement,' is this: "We joy in God, through Our Lord Jesus Christ by Whom we have now received the atonement." (At-*one*-ment) *Reconciliatio* is the Vulgate word, which the King James Version (from which our name was originally derived) translates Atonement in Rom. 5:11.

The first passage that Lewis received on that transformative day pointed to the quickening power of the Holy Spirit. Through the second passage, the Spirit would draw the heart of every future friar into a renewed and energized understanding of Jesus' act of redemptive love. There is no better way to feel the importance of this moment than to read Lewis's own account: "The moment my eyes rested upon the word 'Atonement' it seemed to stand out from that sacred page with a distinctiveness all its own, and it flashed upon me, as I believe from heaven, that the community God was preparing was to be called the Society of the Atonement." This precious moment would mark him forever.

Third Atonement Text
Blood of the New Covenant

✥✥✥✥✥

A third time he opened the Bible, and his eyes fell upon another letter from St. Paul, the eleventh chapter of the First Letter to the Corinthians. These words point to the Holy Sacrifice of the Mass, by which the Atonement of Christ is perpetuated:

For I have received of the Lord that which also I delivered unto you, that the Lord Jesus the same night in which He was betrayed took bread: and when he had given thanks, he brake it, and said, Take, eat: this is my body, which is broken for you: this do in remembrance of me. After the same manner also he took the cup, when he had supped, saying, This cup is the new testament in my blood: this do ye, as oft as ye drink it, in remembrance of me. For as often as ye eat this bread, and drink this cup, ye do shew the Lord's death till he come (1 Cor 11:23-26).

Fr. Paul's Eucharistic contemplation would often focus on the "blood of the covenant." In the Hebrew Scriptures the covenant between God and God's people is sealed with the blood of animals. In the New Testament the covenant is sealed with the precious Blood of Christ. It was his own blood, poured out on the cross, which brought about our redemption.

Five years later, when Lewis and Lurana exchanged crucifixes on Covenant Day, they recalled Jesus, who is our covenant meal and our risen covenant representative. Every time we receive Jesus in the Eucharist we partake of the covenant meal in sacramental form at the altar of sacrifice.

With these living words of Scripture, God fired the faith of Lewis Wattson. He was thirty years old.

After he had received the texts, Father Wattson hastened from the church to the rectory, entered his study and very carefully wrote down the three texts. As he did so, an interior voice, like that which had called him twenty years before, told him that he would have to wait seven more years for his dream of a new religious community to be realized.

2

Chapter Two

A Woman of Valiant Faith

As the deer longs for flowing streams,
so my soul longs for you, O God.

Psalm 42:1-2

G raymoor's co-founder, Mother Lurana White, was born on April 12, 1870, at 33 E. 22nd Street in New York City. Lurana Mary White was born to Francis Steele White and Annie Mary Wheeler White. Her father was an Episcopalian; her mother had been raised in the Dutch Reformed Church. The couple worshipped together in the Episcopal Church after they were married.

Lurana White
and her mother

The new baby soon fell victim to *cholera infantum*. She tossed in her cradle, close to death. Annie White did all in her power. The distraught mother hoped for a skilled nurse to help baby Lurana. She relied on prayer.

The answer to that prayer was a young Irish mother. This woman nursed Lurana with intense devotion. Her love, care, and prayers saved the sick baby. In later years Mother Lurana wondered whether her Irish Catholic nurse had somehow imparted her faith to the child in her charge.

Remarkable Gifts

Lurana displayed remarkable gifts at a young age. Baptized at the age of three in Christ Church, Warwick, New York, on June 22, 1873, she later wrote:

Lurana at 23

I was a very small child, and still believe that I distinctly remember the ceremony. My only sister, Annie Elsie White, was baptized on the same day, she being about 18 months old. I have maintained from the time that I remember also having suffered anxiety beforehand from a feeling of fear lest my little sister should cry when the water was poured on her head. However, she did not.

Already blessed with keen awareness far beyond her years, she also received the gift of reason at an early age. Lurana reminded herself that God spoke directly to Samuel while he was yet a child. And John the Baptist, while yet in Elizabeth's womb, was stirred to jubilation at the greeting of Mary, who carried Jesus in her womb.

At seven, Lurana surprised her beloved grandmother and offered a glimpse into her own faith-filled heart. Her grandmother felt it was time to tell the child about Santa Claus. Lurana had been a serious devotée of St. Nick. When Grandma broke the news that Santa was a story, Lurana was hysterical. Grandma tried to console her, but she sobbed endlessly. When the storm was spent, Grandma held her close and asked, "Why, honey, why cry so hard?"

Lurana searched Grandma's eyes and said, "Because this must mean that Jesus is not real, either!" It was not the loss of Santa. This seven-year-old felt that she had lost the Lord she had come to know and trust.

A Wholly Dedicated Life

✧✧✧✧✧

When she was twenty-three, a powerful lecture on the Sermon on the Mount made a profound impression upon her. She heard the preacher say,

> There may be before me a young woman or a young man who secretly and half fearfully is entertaining the idea of a wholly dedicated life, the oblation of herself or himself to God. I adjure you, be brave and bring that beautiful desire to the light and acknowledge it before God, to yourself and to others. There have ever been and there shall always be some souls who are not content with anything less than a literal fulfillment of these divine counsels.

Lurana shocked her parents with her intention to join the Sisters of the Holy Child, an Episcopalian order with a convent in Albany.

Her yearning for corporate poverty, however, could not be fulfilled there. Lurana had heard of Rev. Lewis Wattson. In her quest for information about an Episcopalian Community where she might live her ideal of poverty, she wrote to him.

She also took decisive steps in that direction. She traveled to London for training among the Sisters of Bethany, with the intention of forming a Franciscan community in the Anglican Communion. After receiving a brown habit, she sought further inspiration in Assisi and in Rome.

*Lurana White
as a postulant
in the Anglican sisters
of the Holy Child*

The Terrace, the White family home in Warwick in New York

27

Possessing a keen logical mind in her formative years, she demonstrated a capacity for quick yet prudent decision-making and a strong devotion to duty. These qualities combined to prepare her for the foundation of a new religious community.

Young Lurana White

From the time of their first correspondence, three years elapsed before Lewis Wattson and Lurana White would meet. Meanwhile, their letters developed their spiritual friendship. They parallel those classic pairs of holy men and women, St. Francis and St. Clare, St. Benedict and St. Scholastica, and others who, together, would show the world its hidden heart, God. At a later point in their joint mission, Rev. Wattson wrote to Mother Lurana:

Lewis Wattson as an Anglican priest

The fact that we should be so entirely of one heart and one soul in our spiritual vision is the striking proof of itself that our inspiration and illumination comes from the same Divine Source as no one fully understands either of us save GOD, and I trust our patron saints. We are being drawn into the deeper recesses of the Sacred Heart....

Miss Julia Chadwick (pictured in later life) and the Elliott sisters restored St. John-in-the-Wilderness Church. They invited Mother Lurana and Rev. Lewis Wattson to minister to Episcopalians there.

The Elliot sisters

St. John-in-the-Wilderness Church

Franciscans, Both

> *Two are better than one,*
> *because they have a good reward for their toil.*
> *For if they fall, one will lift up the other;*
> *but woe to one who is alone and falls*
> *and does not have another to help...*
> *And though one might prevail against another,*
> *two will withstand one.*
> *A threefold cord is not quickly broken.*
>
> *Ecclesiastes 4:9-10, 12*

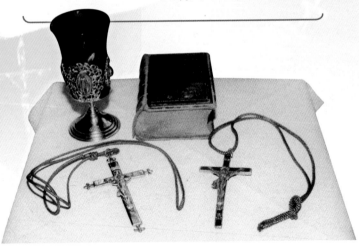

The crucifixes Lewis and Lurana exchanged on Covenant Day

The future founders first met at the White home in Warwick on October 3, 1898, the Feast of the Transitus, commemorating the "passing" of St. Francis. Mother Lurana recorded in her memoirs:

> Our Father arrived in Warwick toward evening, on October 3, the eve of St. Francis' day. On that memorable day we met for the first time. The future Father Founder told the story of his call and of his hopes, and I told him of my search for St. Francis and Corporate Poverty. Then there came to us both the dawning realization of the oneness of God's call.

They spent three days in silence, clearing their minds to receive God's guidance. Singly and together, they prayed before the Blessed Sacrament in their makeshift chapel in Lurana's family home. God instilled in them a divine passion for Christian unity.

The Altar of the Atonement of Graymoor

Covenant Day

October 7, 1898, is forever remembered by the Friars and Sisters of the Atonement as Covenant Day. It was a beautiful fall morning. The air was crisp. The autumn leaves were beginning to turn. The days of prayerful discernment came to a climax in a simple ceremony during a communion service. Mother Foundress described it this way:

> Father blessed and laid on the little improvised altar in the oratory two crucifixes; one he gave to me, the other he kept for himself. The latter had been brought by me from Assisi and I had seen it in the Sacro Convento lowered down until it touched the tomb of St. Francis. It was well understood by the Father Founder and by me that these same crucifixes represented the entire oblation of ourselves into the hands of God, for the purpose of founding the Society of the Atonement.
> Giving all for All!

United in spirit, Lewis and Lurana had found a model and mentor in the Poverello of Assisi, St. Francis. Even as Episcopalians, they embraced Franciscan values and manner of life: conversion; contemplation; trust in God's abundant goodness and love; humility, poverty and simplicity; and a sense of kinship with all life in a divine family.

Like the young Francis Bernadone and Clare Ofreduccio, both experienced transformations that prepared them for their

Mother Lurana

shared mission. Francis had found a new freedom when he left behind the security and comfort of his social status to care for lepers and the poor, even to spend time with them and eat with them.

Turning toward Christ

✥✥✥✥✥

Like Clare of Assisi, Lurana came from a wealthy family. Her grandfather had been the president of Grocers' Bank in New York. His house was the first in New York City to be lighted by gas. Her childhood must have been her pride and the envy of many. But something changed as Lurana grew up. An interior movement of the Spirit turned her away from status, comfort, and possessions and toward Christ. As she later recounted, "Even before I had any definite idea of a religious vocation, I had resolved to separate myself from all things that *appeared* to be necessary – save only Our Lord." [Emphasis added.] At twenty-three she heard the sermon which would catalyze that resolve into action.

Two years later, as a novice of the Sisters of the Holy Child, Lurana read a biography of Francis of Assisi. No doubt she resonated to his love for all God's creatures, a tenderness that had surfaced in her early childhood care for small animals. The saint modeled her ideal of separation from material possessions. At the same time, her work in the sisters' hospital and among the poor in Albany's Episcopal Cathedral Parish put a very human face on poverty. Eventually Lurana would embrace a life of voluntary evangelical poverty that enabled her to understand the circumstances of the marginalized and the poor. With this new clarity, she and her sisters would reach and change many hearts.

Transformation for Mission

Like St. Francis, Lewis Wattson was inspired by the Gospel. He embraced poverty so completely that he swore never to touch money, literally following Jesus' precept to His disciples: "Behold, I am sending you like lambs among wolves. Carry no money bag..." (Luke 10:3-4). He would depend only on God.

His transformation came slowly, step by step along his spiritual journey.

Loyal to his Anglican Communion, Father Wattson experienced darkness as he followed the Gospel's call for unity. Yet in the darkness he discovered light. Early in his ministry as an Episcopalian, Father Wattson had a reputation as contentious. He could argue his point to a fault, often defending principles at the expense of persons. "I need to get down to the very roots of pride and self-will," he acknowledged in an 1898 letter to Mother Lurana. Grace gradually transformed his hearing and seeing, his mind, and his spiritual focus toward unity. His steps turned to a road of peacemaking: he would be able to

Stained glass from friars' parish, St. Joseph, Tsurumi, Japan

resolve conflicts through his intimate understanding of divided Christendom.

Transformation... conversion of heart. These graces, and his cooperation, were not merely matters of personal development. They were God's way of preparing an instrument suitable for the particular work that was to be entrusted to Fr. Lewis and to his spiritual family. Unity does not mean the imposition of one's own way. It requires the capacity to listen, to change, to grow and to receive all that is good in the other.

Just as Francis stripped off all expectations of earthly prosperity and the values of his earthly father, baffling even (especially) Church officials, these future founders abandoned all vestiges of worldly status to blaze a trail for Christian unity. Their mission would evoke misunderstanding, questions, suspicion and even persecution. Francis bore in his body the marks of Christ's wounds, the stigmata. The Atonement founders were also marked, interiorly. As G.K. Chesterton observed, people who are "signed by the Cross go daily into the dark." From painful experience, Fr. Paul could later encourage the Society's members to pray "that God would send down into your hearts ever increasingly the divine love, a flame which urges us on, and makes each able to do things that otherwise would be difficult."

Communion cross in
Mother Lurana's bedroom

Like Francis and Clare, Lewis Wattson and Lurana White responded to the Gospel in a way that challenged the social and ecclesiastical categories that defined many people. Former friends and colleagues kept their distance from these two. Like Francis and Clare, Lewis Wattson and Lurana White trusted the Word of God as the source of divine guidance. This inner conviction freed them from the constraints of social pressures.

Rooted in the Gospel, their Franciscan spirit was not nostalgia for an earlier century; they responded to the needs of their time as fully as St. Francis had to his. From his parents' home, his father's textile business, war's cruelty and the degradation of being a prisoner of war, Francis had internalized life's lessons. Responding to contemporary conflicts, in 1219 he crossed enemy lines during the Fifth Crusade to speak to Sultan al-Kamil. Their conversation ended with a meal, after which Francis and Brother Illuminato returned home "with signs of honor."

Lewis Watson too was a man of his era. He was born into wartime and lived to see two World Wars. As Fr. Paul of Graymoor, he shared the increased Marian devotion inspired by Our Lady's apparitions to three young people at Fatima (1917). He saw the potential represented by the first religious radio station in the United States, KFUO (AM), founded by Lutherans in 1924. These and other twentieth-century events would shape his pioneering mission. He responded to the world's need for healing and reconciliation by his preaching and by the radio broadcasts of the "Ave Maria Hour." With funds raised by The-Union-That-Nothing-Be-Lost, established in 1911 to gather sacrificial offerings, Fr. Paul reached out to missionaries around the world.

United in Trust

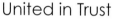

Christ's desire for unity and Mary's role in leading God's people to the heart of her son would be keynotes of Lewis's life and his vocation. These convictions were equally strong within his soul-mate and co-worker, Lurana White.

Walking together in trust, the founders strengthened each other. Scripture says that a cord of three strands is not quickly torn apart. By twining

Fr. Paul's Covenant crucifix and prayer book

together their prayers for each other and for their newly fledged community, they would stand their ground, withstand storms, trials, temptations, and even betrayals and maintain their authentic, unique vocation.

The motivation and driving force to accomplish their goals sprang from their trust in Christ's promises, the foundation of all apostolic faith.

On Covenant Day in 1898, they did not know what lay ahead. The father founder would recall, "During that ceremony we had a great feeling of exaltation and confidence that it was according to the Divine Will." But his confidence would soon be shaken.

The Covenant Promise
✧✧✧✧✧

After the communion service on that first Covenant Day, Father Wattson descended the stairs to the guest room. As he passed through the hall, doubt assailed him: Am I Spirit-led or am I spirit-duped? Should I enter the Roman Catholic Church and join one of its religious orders? Am I a fool for taking on the responsibility of founding the Society, for guiding and advising Sister Lurana, and for promising not to receive a parish salary? By the time he had reached the room and closed the door, his anguish was intense. Sweat began to bead his brow. He fell to his knees, crying out, "Lord, I have no other desire but to do your will. Open the door that you want opened for me. In your gracious kindness, give me a sign so that I may know the way." With that, his eyes fell on Lurana's Bible. He opened its pages to the Letter to the Hebrews:

When God made a promise to Abraham, because he had no one greater by whom to swear, he swore by himself, saying, "I will surely bless you and multiply you." And thus Abraham, having patiently endured, obtained the promise... When God desired to show even more clearly to the heirs of the promise the unchangeable character of his purpose, he guaranteed it by an oath, so that through two unchangeable things, in which it is impossible that God would prove false, we who have taken refuge might be strongly encouraged to seize the hope set before us (Hebrews 6:13-18).

Father Wattson's soul was filled with utter joy! As though seeing a beautiful rainbow in the sky after a severe storm, he had received God's promise! After enduring inner struggle, now he had received assurance that was divine, not from himself or his own ego desires, but from God himself through his Word!
In a letter to Mother Lurana dated October 16, 1898, Lewis wrote:

Of all the gracious acts of Divine Providence which have been showered upon me from the day I was born, nothing has been more marvelous or so exceedingly precious in my eyes than this wondrous message of Divine favor on the Society of the Atonement... O God, establish us in the truest humility and entire dependence on Thee, that our faith fail not!

The assurance given by God's Word so consoled him that, almost forty years later, he wrote on October 7, 1937:

Let those that are just standing on the threshold of the Institute or those who have recently entered into it, be strong in their faith and always remember this Covenant Promise, remember that it is impossible for God to lie who not only made a promise, but confirmed it by an oath that, blessing He will bless the children of the Atonement, and multiplying He will multiply them, as he multiplied the seed of Abraham, until they became as the stars in the firmament and the sands by the seashore that cannot be numbered.

The "Covenant Hymn" written by Fr. Paul remains a treasured reminder of the moment of confirmation that put the future founders' hearts at rest and strengthened them in the storms that would inevitably come.

O God, Who makest Covenant,
Whose promise Thou wilt never break,
Make strong Thy servants militant
With faith and love no pow'r can shake.

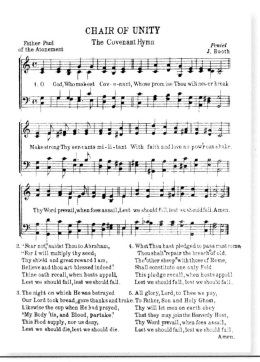

CHAIR OF UNITY
The Covenant Hymn

Father Paul
of the Atonement

Peniel
J. Booth

1. O God, Who makest Cov-e-nant, Whose prom ise Thou wilt nev-er break

Make strong Thy ser-vants mi-li-tant With faith and love no pow'r can shake.

Thy Word prevail, when foes assail, Lest we should fall, lest we should fall. Amen.

2. "Fear not," saidst Thou to Abraham,
"For I will multiply thy seed;
Thy shield and great reward I am,
Believe and thou art blessed indeed".
Thine oath recall, when hosts appall,
Lest we should fall, lest we should fall.

3. The night on which He was betrayed
Our Lord took bread, gave thanks and brake,
Likewise the cup when He had prayed,
"My Body 'tis, and Blood, partake."
This Food supply, nor us deny,
Lest we should die, lest we should die.

4. What Thou hast pledged to pass must come,
Thou shalt repair the breach of old,
The other sheep with those of Rome,
Shall constitute one only Fold
This pledge recall, when hosts appall,
Lest we should fall, lest we should fall.

5. All glory, Lord, to Thee we pay,
To Father, Son and Holy Ghost,
Thy will let men on earth obey
That they may join the Heavenly Host,
Thy Word prevail, when foes assail,
Lest we should fall, lest we should fall.
Amen.

4

Chapter Four

Foundation Day – December 15, 1898

> *When I use the pronoun 'we' and 'our' in regard to the Society of the Atonement, I also included the Sisters... without whose knowledge and consent no important step should be taken lest our house fall through division. Unity, that is, Atonement with God and with each other through Christ and by the Holy Spirit, is the very foundation rock of our Society.*
>
> Letter from Rev. Lewis Wattson to Sister Lurana White

Cold blasts of wind blew down from the hills as the valiant Mother Lurana—after this day, always called "Mother"—and two traveling companions arrived by horse and sleigh to a place along the Hudson River called Graymoor. Here she would found the Franciscan Sisters of the Atonement. Ice build-ups and frosty snow banks did not deter Mother Foundress, who saw a divine purpose beyond the weather.

Several devout Episcopalian women had restored the small church of St. John-in-the-Wilderness Church in a place they named Graymoor; they sought religious to serve there. Just three weeks ago, Mother Lurana had faced the question, "Is this the time to begin?" She had sought God's guidance in Scripture, and the answer had come from the Book of the Prophet Isaiah:

> *Your ancient ruins shall be rebuilt; you shall raise up the foundations of many generations; you shall be called the repairer of the breach, the restorer of streets to live in* (Isaiah 58:12).

The prophet's words carried a commission: to rebuild, to repair a break, to restore. She would accept the commission and launch the work of at-one-ment.

The Road to Foundation Day

✧ ✧ ✧ ✧ ✧

Now it was December 15, 1898, Foundation Day. As she approached the Diamond House, a vacated farm cottage, to take up residence, Mother Lurana's thoughts flashed back over the years that had led to this historic moment. A powerful

The Diamond house

sermon delivered in 1893 had moved her in the spirit of St. Francis, drawing her to imitate him by giving everything to God. In 1894 she had astonished her parents by entering the Sisterhood of the Holy Child. Shivering in the frosty air, she remembered those moments.

Yet her heart had sought still more. She remembered obtaining permission to write to the Reverend Lewis T. Wattson, reputed to be deeply spiritual, of very high Episcopal Church tendencies, and tenacious of Catholic teaching and ritual. Sharing with him her admiration for St. Francis, she had written, "Do you know of any Community in the Episcopal Church vowed to Corporate Poverty?" In their ensuing correspondence they had laid bare the supreme desires of their hearts.

Now Mother Lurana recalled Lewis's words written the year before:

> Step by step I have been led by the unerring Hand of Him 'Whose Providence ordereth all things in heaven and on earth' until at the present time I find myself at the head of a religious household of priests and deacons [in Omaha, Nebraska], that is as clay in the hands of the Divine Potter to make of it whatsoever He pleases. I believe that I shall not be disappointed in my hope that in the course of a very few years 'The Society of the Atonement' will be as much a fact as the Order of the Holy Cross.

It was she, not the priests of Omaha, who would collaborate in that vision. The journey had brought her to this moment, the foundation of a new Franciscan community in the Episcopal Church. It was a leap of faith.

As the wind howled, more memories flooded over her. She was determined to found "a band of mission Sisters called after Saint

Franciscan Sisters of the Atonement in various stages of formation, 1938

Francis, if that might be, doing only mission or parish work and vowed to Corporate Poverty." Thoroughly trained in religious life by the Sisters of Bethany, she had the strength and determination to lay the foundation for a new community.

The Hudson highlands were covered in snow as Mother Lurana stepped from the sleigh. Frigid temperatures did not make the beginning of Graymoor easy, she exclaimed. Yet she knew joy. As Mary replied *"Fiat"* (Let it be done) to the Archangel Gabriel's announcement that she was to give birth, so the foundress of the Society of the Atonement assented to God's will for her and the life she would bring forth.

Founder to Founder – A Letter

✢✢✢✢✢

Within the folds of her Franciscan habit, Mother Lurana held most carefully a letter from Father Wattson written for this occasion, dated December 15, 1898. The future father founder's training with the Episcopalian Order of the Holy Cross kept him in

Westminster, Maryland, on this momentous day. His remarkable letter gave her strength and warmed her heart.

> Well Beloved in the Lord, Greetings:
> For the love I bear the Society of the Atonement, and that I may the more wisely direct the children that God hath given and will give me in it, I have, as you know, placed myself in the hands of the Order of the Holy Cross to be trained by them in the Religious Life. Being, therefore, a prisoner in spiritual bonds, I may not be present at Graymoor to unite with you in the laying of the cornerstone of the convent of St. Francis. But my heart and soul are with you in joyous faith and most fervent prayer.

Looking around her new home, she remembered other words in that letter, anticipating a future reality:

> In the convent of St. Francis, an altar and tabernacle are to be erected to the worship of the Triune God. Upon that altar (the Lord willing it) the all prevailing Sacrifice of the most hallowed Body and Blood of Jesus Christ shall be daily offered: and within the tabernacle the Blessed Sacrament will be perpetually reserved… as the Graymoor nuns kneel in adoration before Him, interceding for all mankind. He will hearken unto their requests. So these holy women, through their power with God in the Most Holy Sacrament, shall bless with the benediction of prayer the very ends of the earth.

Motivated by a strong faith and a willing obedience to God, these two hearts became one heart, though separated by many miles on this historic Foundation Day.

Convent grounds, c. 1930s

The convent complex today embraces
St. John-in-the-Wilderness Church.

5
Chapter Five

Gold Tried in the Furnace

> *I can do all things*
> *through Him who strengthens me.*
>
> *Philippians 4:13*

L ewis T. Wattson was no stranger to pain. Hateful criticism was heaped upon him by those who did not understand his call to preach unity or to live the Franciscan ideal. Besieged by opposition, contradiction and frustration, he suffered but did not falter. Suffering came from within as well, in the spiritual anguish that followed the eventful exchange of crucifixes on Covenant Day. God's word—*"I will surely bless you and multiply you."*— supported him through the many sufferings that lay ahead. God strengthened a trust that would, according to a popular phrase, "turn stumbling blocks into stepping stones."

The Mount of the Atonement

✧✧✧✧✧

On October 3, 1899, Lewis wrote enthusiastically about his arrival at Graymoor. It was exactly one year after he had first met Mother Lurana at Warwick.

The fall colors lifted his heart. Reds, golds, yellows. The sun shone through the leaves. He climbed to the summit of a nearby mountain. The vista over the Hudson River Valley stunned him. The landscape was a patchwork of colors. Words rose from the depths of his silence: "Upon this mountain will rise the monastery home of the preaching Friars. From these heights the prayers and works of reparation of countless Friars of the Atonement

This old paint shed was Fr. Paul's residence until St. Paul's Friary was built. Echoing St. Francis, he called it the "Palace of Lady Poverty."

shall daily ascend to the throne of the mighty Lord of heaven and earth, beseeching His mercy and clemency...." A mighty stream of events would issue from that moment and that decision. A dream was planted in this spot with the holy boldness that comes only from the Spirit of God.

St. Francis Chapel and St. Paul's Friary crown the Graymoor complex on the Mount of the Atonement.

Dedicating a mountain which he did not own was an act of profound trust. Such was his confidence that his call was God-given. The following May, the deed came to him as the result of a seemingly chance intervention. Mother Lurana's kindness to Miss Mary Buxton (later to become Sister Mary Clare, S.A.) while crossing the Atlantic in 1898 had renewed the young woman's faith. A grateful Mary, with her sister and brother-in-law Dr. and Mrs. William Taylor, provided $300, the purchase price for the mountain woodland—the priceless gift of Graymoor's Holy Mountain.

Corpus Christi Cross

The Corpus Christi Cross

On June 14, 1900, the Feast of Corpus Christi, Lewis chopped down a tall cedar tree at the foot of the mountain, fashioned it into a cross, and placed it on his shoulder. Again he climbed to the summit. The cross he erected there stands today, treasured by the friars and the sisters of the Atonement, who renew their call to consecrated religious life by remembering this moment in the life of their community. The Corpus Christi cross is a visible representation of Lewis's intention: Repair the Breach!

Flashbacks took him back over the last two years...pouring himself out before the tabernacle...praying for light to see the truth...studying books on the papal controversy...the sudden, overmastering force of conviction on July 5, 1898, that the papal claims were true and that communion with the See of Peter was the unfailing test of Catholicity. God's peace had flooded his soul at that moment. He had burst into the *Te Deum*.

Erecting the Corpus Christi Cross, Lewis recognized how his new-found faith had been blessed. He savored the memory of exhilarating graces, beyond anything he had known before. He felt the rough simplicity of the Franciscan habit that he had begun to wear on January 25. Mother Lurana had designed it. In a few weeks, he would make his vows.

On October 4 she too would make her vows as a Franciscan, for life. What a gift was Mother Lurana! The Mother Foundress! Why even her name, Lurana, could be traced to the root for the Greek word *luo*, meaning *redemption*. Because its root word is related to the idea of a chain being broken, *luo* refers to aspects of the Atonement of Jesus: forgiveness of all sin, deliverance of the human person from bondage, and the freedom wrought by God's Spirit.

Symbolizing faith, hope and love, the star was worn by both friars and sisters beneath the crucifix.

6

Chapter Six

Light the Lamp

We have been called to heal wounds,
to unite what has fallen apart and
to bring home those who have gone astray.

St. Francis of Assisi

Episcopal priest and Franciscan friar. Rev. Lewis Wattson and Fr. Paul James.

Embracing the new name "Paul James," Lewis T. Wattson professed religious vows atop the Mount of the Atonement, under a white tent erected next to the Corpus Christi cross, before Episcopal Bishop Leighton Coleman of Delaware. It was July 27, 1900. After seven years of yearning, the promises of his three Covenant texts were being fulfilled. (He added the name "Francis" in October.)

The Lamp February 1903
Volume 1 No 1

But suffering had not ended. Fr. Paul was labeled an earnest but erratic priest by the Protestant Episcopal Church, a leper to be shunned. Pulpits closed to him. But he did not give up his hope for "revival" in the Episcopal Church.

Light in St. Paul's Friary entrance to the chapel

On one occasion, a clergyman tried to drown him out with an exhortation that included the words "Let your light so shine." That very phrase goaded Fr. Paul to let his light shine indeed, through alternate media. He took up his pen, "mightier than the sword," and created a new magazine, *The Lamp*, which began publication in February 1903. He placed *The Lamp* under the protection of the Blessed Mother Mary and her "Seraphic Knight," St. Francis of Assisi. *The Lamp* would radiate Fr. Paul's emerging beliefs and his mission for unity.

Anglican Orders and Papal Infallibility

✥✥✥✥✥

Although still an Anglican, Fr. Paul embraced Cardinal (now Blessed) John Henry Newman's perspective, that the definition of papal infallibility was a logical necessity of revelation, which would be worthless unless we had some sure means of knowing what is revealed. Herein lay a conundrum. In 1896 Pope Leo XIII had declared Anglican orders invalid. Increasingly convinced of the claims of the Catholic Church, but also steeped in the writings of Anglican scholars, Fr. Paul believed passionately in the validity of Anglican orders.

He could not accept Pope Leo XIII's declaration. Indeed, he reserved in his chapel what he believed in good conscience to be "the Blessed Sacrament." He considered the Pope to be infallible only when defining in conjunction with an ecumenical council of the Church. It was the position that had prevailed through most of Church history. He derived consolation from sources that he quoted in *The Lamp* to clarify his view. In an article published in *Ave Maria* magazine, he used bold type for emphasis:

Lamp in
St. Francis Chapel

> He [the Pope] **is very rarely infallible.** ...all papal infallibility means is that the Pope can never mislead the world in regard to what Christ taught and commanded. It is not held that the Pope is infallible in governing the Church. As a Ruler he may fail; as Supreme Teacher he cannot err because of Our Lord's promise.

A Family Divided

Assaults came from all sides as he was perceived with "divided allegiance" in his Anglo-Roman double bind. The stress of that dual loyalty can be seen in his comparison to the experience of a child of divorced parents:

> In all good conscience before God, we conceive our spiritual allegiance to be a divided one; not, we hope, through any grievous fault of our own but because, long before we were born, two things

which God has joined together, man, in the violence of self will and evil passion, unlawfully put asunder. When father and mother quarrel and separate, the children are of necessity confronted with a divided allegiance...there being schism in the household, children, in a measure, become a law unto themselves and balance their allegiance to either parent as wisely as they may...

The metaphor of a fractured family allowed Fr. Paul to frame the problem in terms not of disloyalty but of divided loyalties. This use of imagination to find fresh understanding offered an important method for the work of unity. His capacity for new ways of seeing remains instructive even in the twenty-first century, opening up new possibilities in the on-going work of unity.

With love as fathomless as the ocean for the Anglican Church, his mother, Fr. Paul saw the Spirit of the Risen Christ in her midst. He saw God leading her back to the Father's house, as though through a desert. Fr. Paul saw his own church as "the Anglican branch of the Catholic Church" and always prefaced any argument he brought to the table with "In all good conscience before God."

And we, the sons and daughters...will cling to her always... When the mother, pardoned and reconciled, dwells once more in the Father's House, we will dwell there too, most gladly most joyfully; but we would rather be with her in the desert, fighting her battles and helping our Lord bring her on the homeward way, yes, to die in exile by her side, than disowning her to herd with Peter's sheep, though it were in the greenest pasture and to "lie down beside the still waters of comfort."

This love appears in the brief Rule of the Church Unity Army, a prayer league that Fr. Paul established in 1901. He calls for charity

among separated Catholics as though "we were all once more members of the Household of the Faith."

He could not deny the realities that he had experienced: the life in Christ bestowed in Baptism and shared by Christians in what the Second Vatican Council would later term the many "ecclesial communities." The era's internal and inter-denominational conflicts were often fierce. In swirls of words and in the name of Church, combatants could miss the image of God in one another. Fr. Paul's experience of grace flowing in different "branches" models an openness that is meaningful for today's inter-religious dialogue, which recognizes, in the words of the Council, "a ray of that truth which enlightens all."

Witness to a Great Truth

Homecomings can take many forms. *The Lamp* succeeded in bringing to Episcopalians the compelling arguments they had never seen because they had never read Catholic publications. Through reading this little magazine, many people entered the Catholic Church, led there by Fr. Paul's writings in defense of her claims while he himself remained outside.

When *The Lamp* fell under financial strain, Mother Lurana sent her sisters on begging tours, holding out tin cups to collect alms. Fr. Paul never forgot this loyalty. Today's friars honor the memory of those early times, working together with the sisters for the Kingdom and serving the sisters at their motherhouse in Garrison, New York. Thanks to the sisters' sacrifices, *The Lamp* kept burning brightly.

With each new issue of *The Lamp*, Fr. Paul gained prestige and respect. But criticism also mounted. On April 20, 1903, the *New York Herald* carried a half-page article with the shocking headline:

COURTS MARTYRDOM TO HELP REUNITE
THE ANGLICAN CHURCH WITH ROME

Subtitles read **Father Paul, Episcopal Monk, to be Tried for Declaring Reformation a Mistake / Leo XIII is Supreme / Insists that Rome Will Extend to English Church Privileges Given Eastern Rites.** In this article Fr. Paul was quoted:

> Here to this quiet spot I came as a witness to a great truth, and I am ready for anything–for trial, for martyrdom if need be. Ostracized by the clergy, insulted by many and often reviled, I believe that

> some day, perhaps not in mine, all the Christian Churches will be united under the guidance of the bishop of Rome.

On February 23, 1908, the *New York Herald* featured another article on Fr. Paul, under the headline

PRO- ROMAN EPISCOPALIANS UNITE
TO HAIL THE POPE AS PRIMATE

A subtitle summarized the contents: **Remarkable Movement led by Father Paul to unite Anglicans and Catholics is gaining ground in the United States and is now in full swing.**

The article read, in part:

> Organization in this city...of the Anglo-Roman Union composed of Protestant Episcopal clergymen and laymen who seek reunion with the Roman Catholic Church by recognizing the primacy of the Pope, draws attention to a remarkable situation... Its development...is largely due to the indefatigable work of Father Paul James Francis, a clergyman of the Protestant Episcopal Church, who since 1901 has devoted himself to the realization of the ideal of unity for which he has worked more or less since boyhood.

> He lives in a weather-beaten friary on the top of a mountain near Garrison, New York, from which he issues a magazine devoted to the propaganda and sends literature throughout the country. Occasionally, sandaled and tonsured and wearing the Habit of a Franciscan monk, he goes forth into the world preaching of his hope for unity and then returns to his mountain retreat, there to pray and to work for the dawn of the day of the reunited Christendom.

A dreamer of dreams some call him, and churchmen who believe in the immutability of all things religious speak of him with a smile, yet this Episcopal-Franciscan has sent forth an influence which has a far reaching effect. Evidences of a trend toward his teachings are said to have appeared in half of the Episcopal dioceses of the United States. The work has been carried on without display, and even now 'Father Paul,' as he is usually called, deplores the publicity which his plans have gained.

The Lamp would continue its mission of promoting unity until many of its functions were absorbed by *Ecumenical Trends* in 1974. As Fr. Paul and the Society integrated themselves into the Roman Catholic Church after 1909, *The Lamp* also rallied support for world missions and the needs of the universal Church.

7
Chapter Seven

Impulse toward Reconciliation

> *Christians cannot underestimate the burden*
> *of longstanding misgivings inherited from the past*
> *and mutual misunderstandings and prejudices.*
> *Complacency, indifference, and insufficient knowledge*
> *of one another make the situation worse.*
>
> Blessed Pope John Paul II (Ut Unum Sint, Introduction, #2)

As the young community grew up around its founders, the dream of their unity vocation was fast becoming tangible. Men and women sought to share community, poverty, and mission in the Society of the Atonement. Sisters began to fill the Convent of St. Francis next to St. John-in-the-Wilderness Church. More slowly, after Brother Anthony Wallerstein, aspiring friars came, though few stayed in the first years of the small friary that rose atop the Mount of the Atonement.

Atonement sister with kindergarten children, St. Clare's Church, Kawasaki, Japan

The Vocation of Unity

Mother Lurana trusted the Word of God to shape her community of sisters. The Prophet Isaiah's affirmation, "You shall be called the repairer of the breach..." (Isaiah 58:12) gave them their mission. They would work in the service of unity, teaching in parishes and working among the poor, the dispossessed and the broken-hearted. Their charism would touch many, as they embodied Fr. Paul's vision:

> See how God has impressed the vocation of Unity upon us... You are to help souls to be made at one with God, and strive to bring them into personal unity with Him by means of the Church and her Sacraments. Moreover, your struggles and your sufferings, too, will be the combat against whatever opposes itself to this end. We must be prepared for this Crucifixion, for we, too, will share the contradiction of sinners against Himself. Bear witness for these deep things, wrought for souls by Our Lord's Atonement on the Cross...and you will enter into this inheritance and you yourselves will be treading joyfully that path which increases more and more until the perfect day.

Sister Dolores D'Aloia, S.A. lights the Paschal candle during Mass at Sacred Heart of Jesus Church in Rio Verde, Brazil, on April 15, 2012. Fr. Rosimar da Silva Aguiar, the celebrant, was received as an Atonement associate, along with three other candidates.

Atonement sister caring for a baby at New Hope Manor, New York, 1970s

Meanwhile, in the solitude of Graymoor, Fr. Paul prayed for more light as he studied the claims of Rome. Emerging from prayer and study, he became firmly convinced of these claims and of the unique call of the Society of the Atonement: to repair the 16th-century breach between the Church of England and Rome.

Fr. Paul began to urge Anglicans to seek corporate unity with the Holy See. Before his audiences, he called it a madman's dream to contemplate a united church without a visible head. He pressed them with convincing logic. Did not Peter receive the supreme primacy of being the chief shepherd of the Church from Jesus himself? A permanent head and universal shepherd? Yes! Was this not the will of the divine Founder? Look at scriptural passages such as Matthew 10:2 and Matthew 16:18. All bishops must acknowledge the Bishop of Rome as the successor of Peter and be reconciled with him.

The Cost of Prophecy

✧✧✧✧✧

Looking realistically at the looming consequences of such talk, Mother Lurana asked him, "Do you realize to what persecutions, ostracism and peril of annihilation you will be exposing the Society of the Atonement by undertaking such a propaganda?" "Yes," he replied. "I think I do realize quite clearly what a wild and foolhardy proposal it is from the standpoint of worldly prudence. As far as I know, I am the only Anglican ecclesiastic in thirty thousand who holds these views; nevertheless, if our witness is from God, sooner or later it will prevail, though the whole world be against us."

The Chair of Peter at Rome is the divinely constituted center of a reunited Christendom, Fr. Paul steadfastly believed. Therefore he drew up a profession of faith and asked his members for their signatures. Those who could not subscribe to it parted from the Society. The Society of the Atonement was now leaving its moorings in the Anglican Church and venturing toward the Bark of Peter. It was Sunday, October 28, 1900.

Driven by the depth of his belief, Fr. Paul had embraced the identity of a prophet, one who speaks on behalf of God. *"That all may be one…"*: he would be the voice of Christ's prayer for unity, no matter what it cost. Now he was asking the Society of the Atonement to join him as prophets of unity. They would be a light in the darkness of animosity and division.

Fearlessly he proclaimed the message of Christian unity. His unpopularity mushroomed. Close friends, once supportive of his efforts as a religious founder, now distanced themselves and openly opposed him. Even like-minded Episcopalians and Catholics saw him as a dreamer at best. Nonetheless, Fr. Paul was not deterred from preaching church unity on the steps of City Hall and on the streets of New York City, clad in his Franciscan habit.

The secular press took notice. A column in the *Brooklyn Citizen* read:

> A great mountain of difficulty stands in the way of such reconciliation, and only the exercise of the most sublime faith, coupled with the greatest charity, can remove the mountain and cast it into the sea. Yet, with God all things are possible, and the Society of the Atonement believes it can and will be accomplished.

Up and down the Hudson Valley, Fr. Paul preached passionately in Newburgh, Beacon, Kingston and Poughkeepsie. His invitation to Greenport came from a seminary classmate who, with another old friend, became alarmed that Fr. Paul might sermonize on the Pope. They tried to sidetrack him from the topic. As Evening Song began, he was still debating with himself when a clergyman with a trumpet-like voice read a passage from Ezekiel: *"Son of man, stand upon thy feet and I will speak unto thee...whether they will hear, or whether they will forbear (for they are a rebellious house), they shall know that there hath been a prophet among them. And thou, son of man, be not afraid of them, neither be afraid of their words, though briars and thorns be with thee."* This passage resolved his inner debate. He would "follow the Holy Spirit and His Holy manner of working," as St. Francis urged. In silent, earnest prayer, he knelt. Then, with the strength of God, he rose and ascended the steps to the pulpit.

He had been asked to speak on an account in the Acts of the Apostles in which Sts. Peter and John heal a lame beggar at the Temple gate. The healed man leaps with joy, experiencing this sign of God's presence.

Daringly, Fr. Paul compared the lame man to the Church of England, a "lame" product of the English reformation. He posed a rhetorical question: Who was there to strengthen the ankles and feet of the Episcopal Church but the successor of Peter now on the throne of the Fisherman?

The congregation was appalled. One of the attending clergy urged the archdeacon to silence Fr. Paul. Ironically, the archdeacon was the living figure of the lame man, as he had been maimed in a railroad accident. Leaning upon his cane, the lame archdeacon rose and signaled the offertory collection, using the words, "Let your light so shine before men…"

At a subsequent meeting of the archdeanery, Fr. Paul was denounced as a traitor. Such disapproval within his beloved Anglican Communion was painful. However, in later years he would tell the story to his friars with a good sense of humor.

8

Chapter Eight

Apostle of Unity

The Reconciliation of Christians surpasses human powers and capacities. Prayer gives expression to hope that does not disappoint, to trust in the Lord who makes all things new. But prayer must be accompanied by purification of the mind, the feelings and the memory. Thus it becomes an expression of that 'inner conversion' without which there is no true ecumenism...

Blessed John Paul II (Address for the Week of Prayer for Christian Unity, 2005)

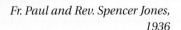

Fr. Paul and Rev. Spencer Jones,
1936

The conviction that the Catholic Church is the living expression of the full Christian tradition continued to drive Fr. Paul.

The Rev. Spencer Jones, an Anglican priest, impressed Fr. Paul with his book on Church Unity, *England and the Holy See*, which the latter considered the most practical and sensible he had read. Their correspondence led to a lifelong friendship. Their synergy for promoting the cause of Christian unity drew others. Their further collaboration, plus the inspiration of Mother Lurana, produced a new volume, *The Prince of the Apostles*.

The Rev. Vincent McNabb, O.P., reviewed the book from a Catholic perspective, writing, "From the first to the last there is hardly a phrase to jar the ears of the most convinced Roman Catholic." And the editor of The Living Church sympathized, "The dreamers are the prophets of better times to come when men of other generations shall be able to realize what these could only dream of."

An Octave of Prayer

✛✛✛✛✛

A letter from Rev. Jones catalyzed the concept of an annual day devoted to sermons on the Pope, followed by prayer. This stirred Fr. Paul's enthusiasm to envision not a day but eight days. The idea of the Church Unity Octave was conceived. Eight days of prayer! What an idea! Fr. Paul felt the anointing of the Holy Spirit. In another moment of inspiration, Fr. Paul chose the time between the Feast of St. Peter's Chair in Rome (then celebrated on January 18) and the Feast of the Conversion of St. Paul (January 25). Its first observance took place in 1908. This week of prayer for Christian unity, fathered by Fr. Paul while in the Episcopal Church, has continued through more than a century. It is like a musical octave in a scale of harmony, the harmony Jesus prayed for: "That they all may be one!" "The intention of this pious observance," said Fr. Paul, was to see the return of "all wanderers to the Unity of the Church and to see all unbelievers led to the Light of the Gospel."

The 1909 observance of the Church Unity Octave broadened the movement toward unity. On October 30, 1909, Cardinal Rafael Merry del Val, Secretary of the Congregation of the Holy Office, sponsored a petition for extension of its observance to the universal Church. On February 15, 1916, Pope Benedict XV, by a papal brief, with the approval of the American bishops, granted that petition. No longer a personal devotion. Now a universal prayer, proper for the entire Church.

Pope Pius XII later renewed the indulgences given through such observance. The Octave swept ahead throughout the world and gained momentum. Through the pages of *The Lamp*, Fr. Paul continued to spread the observance of the Chair of Unity Octave and the acceptance of Petrine claims.

If Fr. Paul were alive today, his involvement with the bilateral discussions on the role of Peter *"primus inter pares"* (first among equals) would have an impact.

UNITY OCTAVE SERMONS

OTHER SHEEP I HAVE THAT ARE NOT OF THIS FOLD THEM ALSO I MUST BRING THERE SHALL BE ONE FOLD AND ONE SHEPHERD S.JOHN X : XVI

The Octave Expands

✧✧✧✧✧

The unity of all Christians moved toward a broader form through the influence of a French Catholic priest, Abbé Paul Couturier, professor of the College de Chartreux in Lyons. His sympathies toward the Russian Orthodox exile community in Lyons motivated him to foster reunion between the Russian Church and the Holy See. So as not to deter Russian Orthodox participation, he observed the Chair of Unity Octave in 1932 in a broader, more ecumenical way.

This approach did not call for Christians to be united under the authority of the Pope. In June 1934, what Couturier called the "Universal Week of Prayer for Christian Unity" was conceived, to be observed during the same time period as the Octave. In this form, Orthodox co-operation with the Octave was immediate. It was first observed in Lyons in 1935. The National Synod of the French Reformed (Calvinist) Church also approved this new form in 1935. In 1940 the World Conference on Faith and Order, an international faith group, approved the Week in its new form. This development reflects the original intention.

Fr. Paul did not want to hinder any movement that would bring together Christians to pray for unity of Christians that "would be pleasing to Christ." His prudence brought him to a new position. He firmly believed that the integrity of faith and Catholic doctrine was fundamental to reunion. Yet he reasoned that when people come together to pray and ask that God's Will be done, because the prayer was situated in the form of what was "pleasing to Christ," he would not be an obstacle.

False notions and deceitful hopes concerned him. He understood that certain issues cannot be passed over in silence or cloaked under ambiguous language. But unity would come in God's timing, manner and intensity, he trusted. Fr. Paul saw reunion under the authority of the successor of Peter as most pleasing to Christ. Looking forward through the lens of faith, Fr. Paul wrote magnificently in the first edition of *The Lamp*:

> Is then Christian Unity a visionary dream? Will the prayer of the Son of God never be answered? Was He a lying Prophet when He foretold the time of its fulfillment, saying: "Other Sheep I have which are not of this fold (the one catholic and Apostolic Church);

them also I must bring and there shall be one fold and one Shepherd." Let who will deride or shake their heads in doubt saying: "Heresy and schism have gone too far; the seamless robe of Christ is too much torn to tatters ever to be mended; the reunion of Christendom is utterly out of the question; Rome is too proud and unbending; England is too self satisfied; the East too orthodox; Protestantism too much enamored of letting everybody do and think just as they please. They never can and they never will come together. Christian Unity is hopeless!"

That they may become one in your hand

Ezekiel 37:15-19, 22-24a

Our answer is, God's Will is Omnipotent; the Fiat of the Most High must prevail; the prayer of Jesus Christ has got to be answered; the Almighty Father would never refuse the dying request of His Only begotten Son; sooner or later every petition of Christ will inevitably be granted. Were the mountains of difficulty to be surmounted a thousand times higher and vaster than they are, God is able to cast them into the sea. Faith serenely rests her case in Him.

Week of Prayer for Christian Unity
2009

9

Chapter Nine

Home Coming
– Reception Day –
October 30, 1909

> *Those who conform themselves*
> *wholly to the divine will, dwell*
> *in a fortress of perfect repose.*
>
> Fr. Paul James Francis, S.A.

The first overtures of the Society of the Atonement to seek corporate admission into the Roman Catholic Church were made in spring 1909. Fr. Paul received a letter from a dear friend, Episcopal Bishop Dr. Frederick Joseph Kinsman (who would enter the Roman Catholic Church ten years later), encouraging him to discharge himself of any dual loyalty and proceed on the road that led to Rome and the Vicar of Christ. On Kinsman's advice, he visited Baltimore's Cardinal James Gibbons in March. The cardinal recommended slow steps, no faster than the Holy Spirit would direct. This message echoed that of Mother Lurana; however, she was the first to approach Archbishop John Farley of New York, with no results.

On August 13, 1909, Fr. Paul met in Washington, D.C., with Archbishop Diomede Falconio, O.F.M., the Apostolic Delegate. Fr. Paul was forty-six years old. He had served in the Episcopal Church in good faith, believing himself a validly ordained priest. In his heart he carried the Atonement texts he had received, Mother Lurana and Covenant Day, the beauty of Graymoor and its river view, the closing of Episcopalian pulpits to him—all this was part of his "salvation history."

Corporate Reception

Now peace flooded his heart as he requested that the Society of the Atonement be admitted *corporately* into the Roman Catholic Church. A warm Franciscan welcome awaited Fr. Paul. Archbishop Falconio helped him to draft a letter (formally dated August 19, 1909) to Pope Pius X. It acknowledged the *jure divino* primacy of the Roman Church and petitioned for the acceptance of the Society of the Atonement in its entirety to submission and Catholic communion. Fr. Paul requested the confirmation of

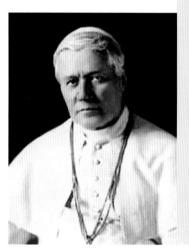

St. Pius X

the Society's name and institute. He requested to hold in trust the Society's motherhouse. By this time the twenty-four-acre Graymoor property included St. Francis House (which he called his "Portiuncula"), the adjoining Mount of the Atonement, and St. Paul's Friary. Archbishop Falconio forwarded the letter to Rome.

Fr. Paul and his fledgling community waited in joyful anticipation of the word that they would be received into the Church and into the Third Order of St. Francis. One morning Fr. Paul confidentially asked Mother Lurana when she thought the Pope's answer would come. She answered October 4, the Feast of St. Francis. Fr. Paul posited that it would come on October 7, the eleventh anniversary of Covenant Day. So it did.

Overcome with emotion, with tears streaming in a joy that rose from his depths, he called together the community and told them of Archbishop Falconio's letter notifying him that the Pope had granted his petition. Cardinal Merry del Val had approached Pope Pius X on their behalf, saying, "Holy Father, please let them in!" The reply from the saintly Pope, who had already been praying for the Society, was swift: "Yes, we will let them in."

The great occasion of the Society's reception was Saturday, October 30, 1909. Seventeen persons—two friars, five sisters, ten tertiaries—corporately entered the Catholic Church and made their profession of faith that day.

From the office of Archbishop Farley of New York came a gold chalice and paten and a missal and missal stand. The gifts were the first of many manifestations of affection from the archbishop. The infant Society of the Atonement was received into the Church by many dignitaries, notably by Fr. Paschal Robinson, O.F.M., distinguished among the Friars Minor as one of the greatest living authorities on Franciscan literature. Ten days later, Fr. Paschal received the friars and sisters into the Franciscan Order.

The End of the Beginning

After a brief period of study in St. Joseph Seminary, Dunwoodie, New York, Fr. Paul was ordained in the Catholic Church on June 16, 1910. Mother Lurana made final vows in her new Franciscan family on November 7, 1911.

Graymoor was "home" at last. Fr. Paul and Mother Lurana had fashioned what Cardinal Francis Spellman of New York would later call "a gem in the court of heaven." This climactic day was a transfiguration experience like that on Mount Tabor. But the Mount of Calvary still awaited them.

Their work for unity had to continue. "Let us begin," said St. Francis, "for up to now we have done nothing."

$$10$$

Chapter Ten

Missionary at Home and Abroad

Come, you that are blessed by my Father...
Just as you did it to one of the least of these who
are members of my family, you did it to me.

Matthew 25:34-40

Fr. Paul's missionary impulse showed itself in particular initiatives, pastoral and priestly and Franciscan, which complemented his work for unity. He believed, "A Society which is consecrated to the...mission of Christ's Atonement, must like the great Church of which it is a very small part, be essentially a missionary organization. Its members must be mission preachers and evangelists, and for that end they must be trained and equipped." This missionary character of the Franciscan family flowed directly from St. Francis. Fr. Paul's zeal and creativity reached around the world in the UNBL and welcomed wanderers into St. Christopher's Inn at Graymoor.

The-Union-That-Nothing-Be-Lost (UNBL) was, in Fr. Paul's estimation, his greatest achievement after the Church Unity Octave. The UNBL would become a providential channel to awaken a missionary spirit among American Catholics and to support the material necessities of missionary efforts throughout the world.

The-Union-That-Nothing-Be-Lost

Chronologically the inspiration for the UNBL preceded the birth of the Octave. On December 21, 1904, Fr. Paul woke up at 5 a.m., hearing in the deepest part of his soul, "Gather up the fragments that remain that nothing be lost," words spoken by Jesus after he had fed a multitude of 5,000 by multiplying five barley loaves and two fish. Fr. Paul thought about the waste and squandering of so many resources that could be used for missionary work.

John Reid, Bro. Philip, T.S.A.

Seven years passed. He submitted a Rule and Constitution for the UNBL to Auxiliary Bishop Thomas F. Cusack of New York in December 1911. Still unsure whether the inspiration was from the Lord, he asked for a sign. The sign came in the form of a shabby old man at the friary door. His name was John Reid (later to become a tertiary member called Brother Philip, T.S.A.). His parents had left him a plot of rocky land in Waterbury, Connecticut. He sold the produce of his small farm, spending the minimum money on himself in order that he might give the maximum to God. John Reid's ardent zeal to establish a trust fund for poor boys who wanted to be priests impressed Fr. Paul, who shared this desire. The farmer promised and sent $5,000 to Fr. Paul for this purpose and included an additional $200. In this gift Fr. Paul saw the "five barley loaves and two fish." The letter in which the money was sent was dated December 21, exactly seven years after Fr. Paul had heard the voice of God in a dream telling him to "gather up the fragments that nothing be lost."

Sisters doing medical mission work and clerical board members of the Catholic Medical Mission Society, meeting in 1925. Through The Lamp, *the UNBL helped support the CMM. Fr. Paul Wattson is second from right.*

Thousands of people enlisted in this missionary union dedicated to the Sacred Heart of Jesus. They followed the call to live simply, making sacrifices for the sake of the corporal works of mercy and the salvation of souls. The UNBL was incorporated under New York State law in 1918. Its funds underwrote the erection of many churches throughout the world. It supported schools, hospitals and other charitable works in Africa, China, Russia, Europe, and the Philippines. Millions of dollars were raised for the expansion of missionary endeavors. Spurred by his love for the medical missions, Fr. Paul appealed through *The Lamp* for funds for medical supplies and medical literature. The Catholic Medical Mission Society became the medical branch of the UNBL. The Graymoor archives hold thousands of letters from around the world testifying to the good done through the UNBL.

His zeal and the generosity of *The Lamp*'s readers found another outlet in The Catholic Near East Welfare Association, which he and others founded in 1924.

Priest and Missionary

This worldwide outreach sprang from Fr. Paul's priestly vocation, which shaped all his activities. Just after he consecrated the elements of bread and wine and before he received Holy Communion, he had placed this inspiration to begin the UNBL in God's hands.

Unwittingly Fr. Paul reveals his own character in his description of a true priest:

> A priest is often called an *'Alter Christus,'* another Christ. It is not only that he daily stands at the Altar and re-presents before the Almighty Father in heaven the oblation of Christ upon the Cross, when He made an Atonement for the sins of the whole world; but in all his life as a pastor of Christ's sheep and a physician of souls, his calling and profession is to live …among the people as another Christ, living the life He lived, going about doing good, consoling the sorrowful, ministering to the poor and the sick, and, if need be, laying down his life in sacrifice for the sheep of his flock…

The spirit of sacrifice fueled his multiple undertakings. His vast correspondence with missionaries around the world, for whom he raised funds, attests to his faith. (This was accomplished without Fr. Paul's ever actually touching a coin or a dollar bill, a vow he had made in 1898.) St. Paul expressed it well: "I can do all things in Him who strengthens me."

Before the Eucharistic Christ enthroned on the altar, Fr. Paul prayed,

> O Lord Jesus Christ, Who commanded Thine Apostles to gather up the fragments that nothing be lost, give us the grace to waste nothing, but to use all our time, talent, substance and opportunity for the greater Glory of God, the good of our neighbor, and the salvation of souls; and all for love of Thee...

St. Christopher's Inn

✣✣✣✣✣

From the centerpoint of Eucharistic adoration, Fr. Paul extended his outreach at home as well. St. Christopher's Inn at Graymoor, founded by Fr. Paul for homeless men, has received much public attention. Steeped in Franciscan tradition, both Mother Lurana and Fr. Paul had great concern and compassion for these "Knights of the Road," as he called them. They honored the dignity of the human person. They knew that Jesus' healing love can transform human brokenness, addictions, and loss of purpose. They trusted that on the Last Day the Risen Lord Jesus will say to the friars and sisters:

> *Come, you that are blessed by my Father, inherit the kingdom prepared for you from the foundation of the world; for I was*

The original St. Christopher's Inn

The original St. Christopher's Inn, upgraded.

hungry and you gave me food, I was thirsty and you gave me something to drink, I was a stranger and you welcomed me, I was naked and you gave me clothing, I was sick and you took care of me, I was in prison and you visited me.... Truly I tell you, just as you did it to one of the least of these who are members of my family, you did it to me (Matthew 25:34-40).

Sketch of Fr. Paul and an Inn resident

Visitors commented on the number of "tramps" that would find their way to Graymoor, treated with the same kindness that the more formal guests received. Fr. Paul dubbed these transient arrivals "Brothers Christopher." One day Fr. Paul and several Brothers Christopher felled some trees to build a chicken coop. A picture of Abraham Lincoln's log cabin birthplace sparked Fr. Paul's imagination: a log cabin refuge for homeless men. The new chicken coop changed its purpose and became the first St. Christopher's Inn.

Throughout the years, men have trekked to Graymoor from all walks of life. Doctors, lawyers, writers, and actors as well as electricians, plumbers and carpenters come to the Inn hopeless and weary, lonely and broken. They might have been crippled by bereavement, pain in the workplace, hunger, sickness, broken

relationships, meaninglessness, failure, physical disability, alcohol or drug addiction, alienation. The Inn's greatest gift may be to see, hear, and understand these sufferers.

Fr. Robert Warren, S.A., and Bro. Raymond Saville, S.A., welcome a new resident to St. Christopher's Inn.

81

At St. Christopher's Inn, the expertise of psychologists and the presence of the Franciscan Friars of the Atonement offer a safe harbor where Brothers Christopher can find healing. Their spirits find balm in the beauty of Graymoor, nestled in the foothills of the Catskill Mountains fifty miles north of New York City, and in the strengths of the staff that engages them in the Twelve Steps of recovery from drug and alcohol addiction.

Many are the stories of these men who have also experienced a spiritual conversion of some kind. Spirituality has helped them to deal with the shock of life's traumas and to dismantle their inner fortresses. Caring support has helped many to discover within themselves a personal truth and the ability to deal with their pain. Through their own openness to a Power greater than themselves, the skills of therapists and the Friars' charity, many of these men have built wholesome lives out of what had seemed wreckage.

"God is on this Mountain,"
a mural in the present St. Christopher's Inn,
was painted by a Brother Christopher.

No matter how hopeless the situation, Fr. Paul believed that God would have the last word. He knew that no one is immune to pain, sickness, and relational or financial problems. All are vulnerable. Extreme suffering turns a person in on himself and destroys the ability to communicate. In such pain, people become "fragmented." Many of the Inn's guests move from

powerlessness and fragmentation. They find ways to express their pain healthily, and their wholeness is restored.

Fr. Paul was a missionary at home as well as abroad. No one is ever turned away from the Inn because of race, religion or sexual orientation. The role of faith is a powerful component of its ministry. Fr. Paul believed in faith's power to liberate. Faith delivers people from loneliness and leads to dialogue. Faith opens up a deep relationship with the divine Other. Faith frees companionship in the search for answers. Faith frees the sufferer from imprisonment in himself to turn to neighbor and God in prayer, worship and fellowship.

The Inn incarnates the reality that there is someone to listen, to help in times of struggle. There are human ears to hear. There are human hands to hold. There are human tears to share. In the midst of suffering, many ask, "Why doesn't God do something?" Fr. Paul believed that God has done something. God has sent us Jesus Christ, who suffered and died for us. God will do more, completing that victory begun on the first Easter Day!

St. Christopher's Inn.

11

Chapter Eleven

Devotion to the Mother of God

> *So closely are the two, Jesus and Mary,*
> *united, that her prayer is always*
> *the echo of the Sacred Heart's desire.*
>
> Fr. Paul Wattson, Retreat meditation 1907

Our Lady of the Atonement
oil painting by G. Martini,
Rome, Italy 1929

Fr. Paul's devotion to Mary, the Mother of God, deserves a chapter in the story of his life and spirituality. He wrote prolifically about her and designed her image as Our Lady of the Atonement. Her blood-red mantle, symbolizing the Precious Blood of the Atonement, gathered his concerns for the infant community and the struggles they would have to endure. He found the purifying fire of God's love through the intercession of Blessed Mary, Queen Mother of the Atonement of Jesus, Queen of Saints and Angels in heaven. Fr. Paul considered her the Society's "teacher."

Fr. Paul was the knight-errant of "Our Lady" and championed her before many of his Protestant friends. "The New Testament is full of her," he pointed out.

Our Lady of the Atonement stained-glass window, St. Francis Chapel, Graymoor

To her God sends the Archangel Gabriel, the Power of the Highest overshadows her, the Holy Ghost comes upon her, the WORD by whom the worlds were made becomes her babe and suckles at her breast; for thirty years Jesus is subject unto her in the home of Nazareth; the first miracle of His public career is performed at her request; she stands by His cross when the disciples save John have fled; one of the seven sayings of Jesus in his agony and death is addressed to her, constituting her to be through eternity the mother of all who should be redeemed by His Precious Blood. Before the last pages of Holy Scripture are written, the veil that hides the glory of the unseen world from our eyes is lifted and "Behold a great wonder in heaven; a woman clothed with the sun and the moon under her feet, and upon her head a crown of twelve stars."

He said further, "The Anglican who pays scant respect to the Holy Mother of God; never says a Hail Mary; has no use for the Rosary... is unfaithful to the oldest and most hallowed traditions of the Anglican Communion." To foster devotion to her among Episcopalians, he and Mother Lurana founded the Rosary League in 1901.

Our Lady of the Atonement

✧✧✧✧✧

Fr. Paul gave Mary the title "Our Lady of the Atonement." His editorial in the March 1910 issue of *The Lamp*, on the Atonement, evokes the presence of Mary at the foot of the Cross, sharing in her Son's sacrifice and purpose:

> What is the Atonement, and why should "the sign manual of God's special love" be the Cross?... That man might be united with God and that this union in its perfection and its bliss might be perpetuated through eternity. That is why Jesus suffered and was crucified and why Mary became Our Lady of the Atonement.

In 1919 Pope Benedict XV granted Fr. Paul's fervent appeal to bless the Atonement Community by recognizing the Graymoor custom of titling the Mother of Christ as Our Lady of the Atonement.

After kneeling before the Blessed Sacrament each night, Fr. Paul would proceed to the altar of Our Lady of the Atonement. There his loving gaze would rest upon the image which he himself had designed—Mary with the moon as her footstool, clothed with the sun and crowned with a diadem of twelve stars, holding in her arms the Christ Child, with a cross in his right hand. The tunic Fr. Paul gave her is blue, and her mantle is blood-red, symbolic of the Precious Blood of the

Our Lady of the Atonement oil painting by Margaret Mary Nealis c. 1933

Atonement. On each side of the image of Mary are two angels holding the instruments of Christ's Passion—the lash, the crown of thorns, the nails, the lance.

Fr. Paul composed a prayer which continues in use by the friars and the sisters of the Atonement.

THE THREE-FOLD SALUTATION

We salute you,
Holy Mary, Daughter of God the Father, and entreat you to obtain for us a devotion like your own to the Most Sweet Will of God.

We salute you,
Virgin Mother of God the Son, and entreat you to obtain for us such union with the Sacred Heart of Jesus that our own hearts burn with love for God, and an ardent zeal for the salvation of Souls.

We salute you,
Immaculate Spouse of God the Holy Spirit, and entreat you to obtain for us such yielding of ourselves to the Blessed Spirit that He may, in all things, direct and rule our hearts, and that we may never grieve Him in thought, word, or deed.

Legacy of Our Devotion

Fr. Paul "lighted" *The Lamp* on the feast of Candlemas (the Presentation of the Child Jesus in the Temple, celebrated with devotion to Mary) in 1903. He and Mother Lurana placed it under the special protection of "Our Immaculate Lady, Queen of Heaven." In his first editorial he called her the "Lamp of Burnished Gold, who came to the Temple bearing the Light of the World."

Fr. Paul left his friars and sisters a great legacy in his devotion to Our Lady of the Atonement. He knew that her role was and is to lead others to the Heart of her Son, Jesus. "Do whatever He tells you," she said at the wedding feast of Cana, when she prompted Jesus to change water into wine. Mary stood at the foot of her Son's Cross, her will united completely to his, her sacrifice joined to his for the one purpose, the salvation of the world. As Our Lady of the Atonement she stands at the center of the Society's vocation and mission.

Fr. Paul rehearses for a 1937 broadcat of the Ave Maria Hour.

The Cathedral of Our Lady of the Atonement in Baguio, the Philippines

Rehearsal for an outdoor broadcast of the Ave Maria Hour from Graymoor

*Fr. Samuel Cummings, S.A.,
delivers a blessing in a studio
broadcast of the Ave Maria Hour.*

*Our Lady of the Atonement statue on
the facade of the Baguio cathedral*

12

Contemplative Spirit

> *We enter into solitude first of all to meet*
> *the Lord and to be with him and him alone.*
> *Our primary task in solitude, therefore, is...*
> *to keep the eyes of our mind and heart*
> *on him who is our divine savior...*
> *Only with a single-minded attention*
> *to Christ can we give up our clinging fears*
> *and face our true nature.*
>
> *Henri Nouwen*

The home of the Franciscan Friars and Sisters of the Atonement is in the foothills of the Catskill Mountains, fifty miles north of Times Square. Fr. Paul and Mother Lurana rejoiced that God had given them this property. In difficult times, the quietness of the woods and the natural beauty of the Hudson River Valley were invitations to prayer and silence. From the nature of creation to the God of creation! For both founders, contemplation was essential.

Fr. Paul on the porch of
St. Louis Hermitage, Graymoor, c. 1920

For them solitude was not a private therapeutic place. It was the place of conversion, the place where the old self dies and the new self is born, the place where the new man and the new woman emerge. In a text for his own meditation, Fr. Paul wrote, "Contemplate JESUS as the King with the Burning Heart. How it is love that impels Him to seek a habitation in my soul and how if He enters He will shed abroad His love within us, until our own hearts burn with the Fire of His Heart."

St. Clare
Hermitage, Graymoor

Both Fr. Paul and Mother Lurana had envisioned a contemplative core within their institute. They knew how important it is for missionary success to have a small number of friars and sisters invited to be a spiritual dynamo in the center of all active apostolates within the community. They planned for a "hermitage." Work started, but it was never finished.

Contemplation weaves through the Society's heritage. Fr. Paul decided that a tiny cottage damaged by wind in 1915 should be restored as St. Louis Hermitage. He treasured the prayerful solitude that the Hermitage allowed him. For the sisters, St. Clare Hermitage, dedicated in 1932, would serve as a retreat when they, as *The Lamp* described it, "for a while desire to retire from their active Missionary life." Mother Lurana and Fr. Paul shared the conviction that a later Atonement sister expressed:

> The contemplative life is our life of prayer - the times we go away from the active, to sit quietly at the feet of Jesus and contemplate the things of God... Both [active and contemplative] life-styles must be ours. The contemplative lifestyle gives the religious the strength, the motivation to go out to the people and serve their every need.

These hermitages were the antecedents of the friars' and sisters' retreat ministries and of today's retreat facilities.

The Blood of Christ

The founders placed a high value on silent adoration before the Blessed Sacrament. Their strength came from Eucharistic contemplation, with an emphasis on the spirituality of the precious Blood of Christ. This is evidenced in Fr. Paul's decision to line the Franciscan scapular with a dark red fabric reminiscent of blood, an idea suggested by Mother Lurana. Before the Blessed Sacrament, in adoration, they were drawn into a deep awareness of God's love.

How many "Holy Hours" did Fr. Paul and Mother Lurana experience? One will never know. Most importantly, they felt it was a privileged time of awareness; they were in the presence of a loving and tender God and were redeemed by the Blood of Christ. This Precious Blood, present for us in the Eucharistic sacrament, is Christ. By the Blood of Christ—by the outpouring of his life and love—God brings us together with him and each other.

They knew well Romans 5:9-11:

> *We have been justified by his blood… For if we have were reconciled to God through the death of his son, much more surely, having been reconciled, will we be saved by his life. But more than that, we joy in God through our Lord Jesus Christ, by whom we have now received the Atonement.*

While in silence before the Blessed Sacrament they were active participants in the offering of the Blood of Christ to the Father. Fr. Paul prayed, "Eternal Father, we offer you the Precious Blood of Jesus, poured out on the Cross and offered daily on the altar." The "offering" of the redeeming Blood of Christ is made to the Father. Jesus, who perfectly complies with the will of his Father, says, *"Father, into your hands I commend my spirit"* (Luke 23:46).

Guiding the friars in meditation on the Eucharist in November 1900, he urged them to "Contemplate the Prince of the Atonement stretched on the altar of sacrifice, dying to reconcile sinners unto GOD." And he asked them to consider, "Am I willing to lay down my life along with His on the cross of sacrifice to further the desire of the Sacred Heart...?"

Contemplative Presence

✧✧✧✧✧

Contemplation, said St. John of the Cross, is a "simple infusion of God's peace, [that] when allowed to enter the shaft of the soul, turns the soul on fire." Both founders bore the torch, the mystery of the Atonement. The silence of their contemplation was a silence bursting with the presence of God. In the words of St. Augustine: "I searched for your face, O God, in all things in all the world; I discovered you within me, in my own soul, in my own heart." Their contemplation was a simple, direct looking at Christ. In the mystery of Love, contemplation is to say to Christ, "Here I am! You are here! Speak, Lord, your servant is listening!"

Fr. Paul in the chapel of St. Christopher's Inn

13

Chapter Thirteen

Fire in the Night

> *As a fire that shines in the night,*
> *so too his life here on earth.*
> Ignatius Smith, O.P. (Eulogy at Fr. Paul's funeral)

As fire shines in the night, Fr. Paul's earthly life brightened his world. That light went out early in the morning of February 8, 1940, after what appeared to be a heart attack.

His courage and determination had given rise to a community dedicated to the heart of Jesus and to his passion for unity and reconciliation. In the service of this mission, scores of men had become friars. Thousands of the faithful had found spiritual renewal on pilgrimages to Graymoor. Fr. Paul's creative use of media extended to the *Ave Maria Hour*, a radio program carrying Christ's message into homes across the land.

Such a charismatic gift is tested in the crucible. Fr. Paul suffered the denial that his Episcopal ordination had validity. He suffered the anger of many former friends and colleagues in his beloved Anglican Communion and the suspicion of many Catholics that he was really a Protestant at heart.

Perhaps his deepest sorrow came with the death of Mother Lurana on April 15, 1935, at the age of sixty-five. Early that morning, Monday of Holy Week, he had been called to her deathbed. She had suffered long, her body "a factory of pain," in her words. Fr. Paul anointed her, then left to offer Mass for the community. He had not yet reached the sacristy when he was called back. She had breathed her last.

The next day the Mother Foundress's body was carried to the small church of St. John-in-the-Wilderness, which had figured in her arrival at Graymoor. There her sisters kept vigil with her before the Blessed Sacrament until the funeral on April 17. During the Mass, the large crowd spilled out of the small church, then joined the procession as friars bore the body to its final resting place in the sisters' cemetery. Miss Annie Elsie White was present, as she had been on Founding Day in 1898.

Fr. Paul treasured Mother Lurana's final message, left in a letter to be read after her death: "If our Lord permits, and I think He will, I will help you and the Institute after my death, and therefore think of me as not far off."

For five more years, the father founder remained to guide the Society. On his seventieth birthday he had written, "I feel that 70 years represents a complete cycle of earthly existence; that I have entered upon a sort of middle ground, or shall we call it, a causeway, between the life that has been and the one that will be beyond the veil. There is much, very

Mother Lurana's bedroom

much to be set in order and transacted ere the final summons comes, but like Enoch I desire to walk more alone with God. This is not being unmindful of the sacred ties of the S.A. They are eternal and never do I forget them..."

On his seventy-seventh birthday, January 16, 1940 (feast of the Franciscan martyrs), he delivered his "Final Testament," an expression of gratitude and sacrifice, praising the martyrs' fidelity unto death. As his earthly life came to an end, his work had not ended. Several fields were tilled and awaiting planting. Others had been planted and were already being harvested.

The Winds Sing

✛✛✛✛✛

Fr. Paul was buried at Graymoor on February 12. His eulogist was his loyal longtime friend, Fr. Ignatius Smith, O.P., dean of the School of Philosophy at the Catholic University of America. Quoting extensively from this eulogy, the author feels this is a fitting tribute to his spirit, which is now even more active in the Franciscan Friars and Sisters of the Atonement.

> The winds sing a dirge on the Mount of Graymoor. In the valley there is peace but a numbing sorrow. The angels of God in the heavens above rejoice that the soul of a saint has come home to the Father. Humanity here is bowed under sorrow that shows in tears streaming down loving faces, not tears of rebellion but from hearts left so lonely by the death of a father and friend. The message of God, in the call of the grim reaper, has called from our midst the soul of Fr. Paul Francis.
>
> To honor his work, to pray for his peace, to console his spiritual family we gather here before his mortal remains, scarcely realizing that he is gone.

The Friars of the Atonement, Brothers and Students are stunned by the trial and the loss they suffer. The Sisters of the Atonement, both here on the Mount and out on the far-flung firing line of Catholic work inspired by Father Paul Francis, are hallowing their grief with their prayers of devotion. The Brothers Christopher, the constant object of his tender affection, are mute in the sorrow imposed by the death of this apostle of charity. Away from these legions who watched o'er his body are thousands of Tertiaries, a hundred thousand members of the Rosary League and of The-Union-That-Nothing-Be-Lost who have learned both to love this champion of the church and to lean upon him for spiritual consolation.

And scattered over the world from Rome to China, from the Yukon to the Amazon, are hundreds of thousands of men, women and children, high ecclesiastics, and humble laity, Protestants, Catholics, Jews and infidels to whom he has appealed and whom he has helped. The Church, the Nation and the ranks of humanitarians have lost an international leader. A place has been left vacant that will never be filled…

Father Paul Francis lived to see his work grow to tremendous proportions. There is no time for me to mention the growth of the Society of the Atonement in physical equipment and resources under his leadership and through his untiring efforts and prayers. Suffice it to say that this bleak and desolate mountain has been turned into a little attractive and populous city of God with numerous buildings and activities, while at the same time bleak and barren hearts and souls have been made attractive and fruitful with the manifold graces of God brought to them through the example and intercession of this other Christ who went about always doing good.

Father Paul Francis lived to see the houses of the Friars and Sisters established in New York, Philadelphia, Washington, Texas, British Columbia, Northern Alberta, Ireland, England, Assisi, and Rome. Into the Catholic Church, when he brought the Society of the Atonement, he led two Friars, five Sisters and ten Tertiaries. He lived to see his number grow, within thirty years, under the Sacramental power of the Catholic Church to 170 Friars, 230 Sisters and 1000 Tertiaries. During the same time he enrolled in the Rosary League and The-Union-That-Nothing-Be-Lost 100,000 persons.

Rivaling this numerical and physical growth of the works inspired by God in the mind and the life of this saintly apostle of poverty, was the growth of the recognition extended to his undertakings by the authorities of the Church. In 1909 the Church Unity Octave was sanctioned and blessed by Pope Pius the Tenth, and in 1916 it was extended to the Universal Church. In 1921, the American Catholic bishops decreed that it should be established in the various dioceses of the United States.

In this way the work as well as the name of Father Paul has become known in every city, town and hamlet of the nation, confirming the fame and advancing the labors of this genial ascetic for the

The mural over Mother Lurana's tomb, Graymoor

salvation of souls through the radio with the Ave Maria Hour and other programs to turn the mind and heart of the nation heavenwards. Truly this was a marvelous career that could have been achieved only by one with a very unusual character.

Fr. Ignatius ended his sermon by stating that

Fr. Paul had the qualities of a great heart with soul-exhausting efforts for the preservation and propagation of the faith. Standing out supreme among the great qualities of his magnanimous heart was courage. It was something of which ordinary men, lay and clerical, stood in awe. It can be explained only when we know of his constant and consuming sense of the living presence of God at all times and everywhere in everything he taught and did. It can be explained, this supernatural courage, only when we understand that here is a man who took Jesus seriously, and lived with Him literally, and was eternally conscious of the Divine Providence of the Omnipotent Creator and Preserver of this universe…

I need not speak again of the spirit of practical charity by which he gave his life to the spiritual and corporal works of mercy and through which so many thousands have been made more comfortable in body and in soul…

Deep down in the foundation of his spirituality was the bedrock of humility, the humility that is possessed only by great souls who know how to be courageous in defeat as well as sober and poised in the midst of remarkable success.

Into the twenty-first century, the spirit of Fr. Paul and Mother Lurana inspires the Friars and Sisters of the Atonement, in ministry on several continents. The Society continues to make its vital contribution to the Church and to the world.

Fr. Paul and Bro. Barnabas Walsh looking out over the Hudson Valley

Fr. Samuel Cummings, S.A., and Fr. Paul at a baseball game between Graymoor's and Maryknoll's seminarians

Éditions du Signe
1 rue Alfred Kastler
B.P. 10094 Eckbolsheim
67038 Strasbourg Cedex
Tél : ++ 33 (03) 88 78 91 91
Fax : ++33 (03) 88 78 91 99
www.editionsdusigne.fr
E-mail : info@editionsdusigne.fr

Publication Director: Christian Riehl
Assistant Publication Director: Anne-Lise Hauchard
Editor: Mary-Cabrini Durkin
Photos: Graymoor Archives and Dan Fisher
© Fotolia: p. 8 and 10: jakezc; p. 38: leungchopan; p. 54, 56 and 58: Jenson

Layout: Sylvie Tusinski

ISBN: 978-2-7468-2950-3
All rights reserved © Éditions du Signe - 2013, 109164
Printed in U.E.